"*Good Pictures Bad Pictures* is the practical, positive, and powerful tool families need. I whole-heartedly recommend reading this with your children regularly so they will develop self-control—the ultimate protection from pornography.

VAUNA DAVIS, EXECUTIVE DIRECTOR OF UTAH COALITION AGAINST PORNOGRAPHY

"I was thrilled to find *Good Pictures Bad Pictures*. As a parent, it makes opening that sensitive conversation as easy and loving as reading a book together. I love everything about it! It's honest and open and calm and reassuring. What a beautiful way to empower and protect your child!"

DEANNA LAMBSON, MOTHER OF 6, TEACHER AND FOUNDER OF WHITERIBBONWEEK.ORG

"I highly recommend *Good Pictures Bad Pictures*. As I read this book to my children it opened up an opportunity to discuss difficult matters. It presents the material in a way that children can relate to and understand."

GREG, FATHER OF 6

"*Good Pictures Bad Pictures* is a book every family needs to read. It has been priceless in helping us start a dialogue with our young children about the harmful effects of pornography."

MARCIA STILLWELL, MOM OF 5

"Reading *Good Pictures Bad Pictures* with my children may be one of the most important things I've ever done for them. I have witnessed the ravaging effects of pornography in the lives of many loved ones, but until finding this book, I didn't know how to begin a dialogue with my young children to help neutralize pornography's powerful vortex of addiction. The book's meticulous word choice; powerful yet simple description of the two parts of the brain; and its "CAN DO" plan (the equivalent of a fire evacuation plan for any internet-enabled device) have given me tremendous peace of mind. I look forward to reinforcing its concepts often."

DIANE, MOTHER OF 6

More Praise for *Good Pictures Bad Pictures*

"*Good Pictures Bad Pictures* is exceptional. It is evidence-driven, targeted and articulate. I will be giving copies to my children to read to my grandkids!"

JAN GARBETT, GRANDMOTHER, 17 YEAR WHITE RIBBON WEEK PTA VOLUNTEER

"The CAN DO Plan teaches essential skills anyone can use to reject pornography!"

ANGELA PAGE, PRESIDENT WOMEN FOR DECENCY

"*Good Pictures Bad Pictures* is a great way to open communication with your children regarding the difficult topic of pornography. It provides a vocabulary we can now use to discuss it (which is extremely helpful to this awkward, tongue-tied mom). Thanks to this book, my kids are now better porn-proofed because they know what to do whenever they see bad pictures!"

JENNY, MOM OF 4

"*Good Pictures Bad Pictures* is an amazing book! I honestly don't know when I would have started this conversation with my kids, but this book made it such a natural way to begin. I read it to my kids (ages 4 to 12—two of whom are also on the autism spectrum). I loved how the book explains the brain with analogies and terms my kids can understand. I feel so much more comfortable that my kids will know what to do when they see bad pictures.

SHANDIIN SCHWENDIMAN

"Your book is a winner! I loved the format—such a great model for any parent-child conversation of difficult topics, and a very comfortable way to open a dialogue about pornography."

CINDY DIEHL, MOM OF 5

GOOD PICTURES BAD PICTURES

Porn-Proofing Today's Young Kids

Kristen A. Jenson, MA and Gail Poyner, PhD
Illustrated by Debbie Fox

GLEN COVE PRESS

TO MY TREASURES: SARAH, LOREN, LILA, SPENCER AND JOHN

—KAJ—

TO GENE, MY FOREVER LOVE

—GAP—

Disclaimer

It is the opinion of the authors that children are safer when they are proactively warned and empowered to reject the dangers of pornography and addiction. However, parents and caregivers are ultimately responsible for how they educate their children about these serious issues. This book does not constitute medical or psychological advice for treating addiction. People suffering from addiction should seek competent professional services. The anecdotal stories we share are true to life, and they are included with the permission of the persons involved.

ISBN: 0615927335

ISBN 13: 9780615927336

Contents

Acknowledgments

It takes a village to produce a book like this! So many wonderful people made crucial contributions. The writings and online video presentations of Donald L. Hilton Jr., MD, helped us explain how the brain can develop an actual addiction to pornography. Specifically, we shared and expanded upon his "ice cream truck" analogy in chapter 5. Special recognition goes to Jill Manning, PhD, author of *What's the Big Deal about Pornography? A Guide for the Internet Generation.* Her work inspired the first four of the CAN DO Plan™ strategies listed in chapter 8. The videos by Gordon S. Bruin, MA, LPC, founder of Innergold Counseling Services, Inc. were helpful as we worked to create simple, kid-friendly explanations of our two brains. Claudine Gallacher, MA, spent hundreds of hours serving as a research assistant and writing coach; her constant encouragement, feedback and help with wordsmithing were crucial contributions. Kristen's neighbors, Jared and Nicole Liebert and their sons, served as models for the illustrations and were early and enthusiastic "guinea pig" readers. Kristen is grateful for all the encouragement she received from her writing group,

The Columbia River Writers, and our chapter's founder, author Tanya Parker Mills, who helped Kristen start her blog, Protect Young Minds. We want to thank Genevieve Ford with Eschler Editing who made great suggestions and helped to polish our manuscript. Most importantly, we truly appreciate the courageous souls who shared with us their stories of early exposure and subsequent addiction to pornography; they gave us deep wells of inspiration and motivation. Additionally, the dozens of parents who served as volunteer test-readers gave us critical feedback that helped us improve and make this book more effective for kids. Furthermore, we applaud all organizations and individuals who are shining a light on the dark and addictive power of pornography; their books, articles, blogs, films, and information on social media sites are making an incalculable difference. A final shout-out needs to go to our husbands and family members who have cheered us on every step of the way—their love and encouragement were sustaining forces for the nearly three years it took to research, write, and refine *Good Pictures Bad Pictures.*

A NOTE FROM KRISTEN ABOUT THE ILLUSTRATIONS

Ten years before we started this book project, my young son passed away. A few months after his death, Debbie Fox brought me a beautiful watercolor portrait of him. She had painted it from the photo on the back of his memorial service program. I count this gift as one of my greatest treasures.

When I asked myself the question, "How do we illustrate a book for kids about pornography?" I knew I wanted the illustrations to be in watercolor. They needed to be classic and

soft to counter the harshness of pornography; and real, not cartoonish—I didn't want to risk trivializing this serious problem.

It was a no-brainer that Debbie was the one to paint the authentic and beautiful illustrations we needed, and I'm grateful she accepted the challenge. She was a dream to work with, showing endless patience and flexibility. We believe her hand-painted artistry makes *Good Pictures Bad Pictures* an even more comfortable and inviting book for parents and kids.

INTRODUCTION

Why We're Not Crazy for Writing This Book

You may be asking yourself, "Talk to seven-year-olds about *pornography*? You've got to be kidding! Shouldn't I wait until they're twelve or thirteen?" We get it. We know that good parents want to protect their kids' innocence. But the sad reality is that many children, all over the world, begin viewing hard-core Internet pornography long before their parents even consider discussing its dangers.

Young children are being exposed to Internet pornography. Consider the eight-year-old girl who received the "sex talk" from her parents and then got an Internet-enabled device for her birthday. Her innocent curiosity about sex prompted online searches, which quickly led to the violent and degraded world of hard-core Internet pornography. Previously a happy and outgoing girl, she became withdrawn and depressed before her mother discovered her porn habit.

A seven-year-old boy was shown a pornographic magazine by his older cousins. After that shocking initial exposure, he felt compelled to seek out more nude pictures though he knew nothing about sex. Later, the Internet provided a slippery slope to decades of addiction.

A six-year-old boy was molested by his foster sister, initiating his premature interest in sex. As a preteen he found Internet pornography. But it wasn't until he was seventeen that his parents found out the devastating truth: he'd been molesting his younger siblings for years, all the while hiding his porn addiction.

These kids are the reason we wrote *Good Pictures Bad Pictures*. After hearing their tragic stories, we searched for a children's book that explained the dangers of pornography addiction, but came up empty-handed. We wrote *Good Pictures Bad Pictures* as a tool to help parents begin a dialogue about

pornography before kids become interested in it and while they still see their parents as a credible source of information. In other words, to play an offensive game against pornography: to get in first and immunize kids against the very real harms of "picture poison."

It's no surprise that kids are so easily ensnared by pornography. Today's Internet creates an unprecedented opportunity to view hard-core pornography. It's *accessible* from any Internet-enabled device, *anonymous*, and *affordable* (so much is free). And even if your child doesn't own a mobile device, he or she very likely has friends who do.

That's why Internet filters are important, but not enough. When it comes to kids and pornography, *ignorance is risk*. We live in a hypersexualized culture, so raising kids with sexual integrity requires early training. Why? A child's brain is more vulnerable to porn because it is designed to imitate what it sees. Additionally, a child's brain has less ability to control those imitative impulses. Viewing pornography can alter the brain's neural pathways and initiate an addiction that is often harder to overcome than drugs or alcohol.

But addiction isn't the only danger. Although not every child will develop an addiction to pornography, virtually 100 percent of kids who choose to continue to view porn after an initial exposure are negatively influenced. Today's Internet pornography goes way beyond the still, nude photos of men's magazines. It has metastasized into a hundred thousand variants of degrading violence, including rape, sex with children, group sex, and horrors we won't even mention here.

Pornography is a *sinister counterfeit*—it teaches kids that sex is a form of self-gratifying and often violent diversion instead of a way to *build a loving and committed relationship* with someone they trust. As a result, kids who consume pornography can become corrupted with unhealthy sexual attitudes and may find it difficult to develop, commit to, or even want a long-term sexual relationship with a real person.

That's why kids must develop their own internal filters. We call it *porn-proofing*: empowering kids by teaching them *what* pornography is, *why* it's harmful to their brains, and *how* they can minimize its impact once they have been exposed. You're going to love the CAN DO Plan™ that we've provided in chapter 8! It features five simple steps that empower your child with the cognitive skills needed to control their thoughts and impulsivity.

Opening a dialogue is crucial. The goal of *Good Pictures Bad Pictures* is to help you begin talking with your kids about the dangers of pornography. For more information about teaching your kids to reject pornography, please join us at ProtectYoungMinds.org, a blog written by author Kristen A. Jenson.

This book is easy to read to kids. *Good Pictures Bad Pictures* uses the comfortable setting of a

mother and son enjoying a family photo album and models a conversation that teaches a simple definition of pornography (even for kids who have not yet learned the details of sex). Chapter by chapter, kids learn about addiction and their "two brains" (the feeling brain and the thinking brain) and how one of them can be tricked by viewing pornography, while the other can take control and prevent addiction.

How the book is organized. The first seven chapters explain what pornography is and how the brain can be tricked into developing an addiction to it. Chapter 8 provides five powerful CAN DO Plan™ strategies for dealing with exposure to pornography. Chapter 9 brings in Dad, who confirms what Mom has taught about the dangers of pornography, and explains how porn can act like a poison. Depending on your child's attention span, this concluding chapter can serve as a final warning or a good way to review major concepts during a follow-up discussion (and we hope you have many of them). Finally, two helpful lists are provided at the back of the book: a glossary of key terms (first occurrences of key terms in the story are in **bold** type) and resources for parents and professionals.

Four tips to maximize the benefit of *Good Pictures Bad Pictures*:

1. Take it slowly. For some kids, reading and discussing the book in more than one session might work best. (Natural breaks occur after chapter 5 and chapter 8.)

2. Encourage questions from your children. If they stump you, it's okay to say, "That's a great question! Let me think about it and get back to you."

3. Feel free to expand upon explanations and use analogies or stories from your own family to clarify concepts. If you've already had the sex talk with your child, it may be helpful to expand the definition of pornography (see the glossary of terms at the back of the book). This book is a tool, and you should decide how best to use it to help your kids.

4. Remain calm. Shame and secrecy only increase the power of porn. If your kids reveal a past exposure to pornography, this is a good opportunity to find how much they've seen, read, or listened to.

Our sincere thanks go to the many parents, children, and professionals who have reviewed, test-driven, and supported this book. We are convinced that given preparation, kids can learn to protect their brains from the devastating effects of pornography and enjoy a healthy and happy future.

KRISTEN A. JENSON, MA, AND GAIL A. POYNER, PHD

CHAPTER 1
What's Pornography?

One Sunday afternoon, Mom and I sat on the couch and flipped through a pile of photo albums. I liked looking at pictures from our trips to the beach last summer and Uncle Adam's wedding last fall.

After we finished, Mom got a serious look on her face.

"There's something I've wanted to talk with you about," Mom said. "Our photo album is full of *good pictures* that remind us of how important our family and friends are. But did you know there are *bad pictures*, too?"

I shook my head. "What do you mean by *bad pictures*?"

Mom closed the photo album and looked at me. "The bad pictures I'm talking about are called **pornography** or *porn*."

"What's poor-nog-gra-fee?" I asked.

"Pornography means pictures, videos, or even cartoons of people with little or no clothes on. Have you ever seen pictures like that?" Mom asked.

I thought about it and then I remembered something.

"I once saw a picture of a naked man and woman in a science book at the library. All of their parts were labeled. Is that pornography?"

Mom smiled. "No, there's a difference between a drawing in a science book and pornography."

She opened up the photo album and pointed to pictures of me and my cousins at the beach.

"Pornography shows the parts of the body that we keep private—like the parts we cover with a swimsuit."

For a moment, Mom stopped to think.

"Most kids who see pornography know immediately that it feels wrong. Some kids say it makes them feel embarrassed or even sick to their stomach."

"Then why do kids look at it?" I asked.

"Pornography is tricky because it can feel exciting to your body. In fact, pornography tricks the brain into releasing a big dose of **chemicals** that make your body feel really good—for a short time. But tricking the brain with pornography can soon lead to big problems."

Mom gently tapped the top of my head with her finger.

"The problem is that pornography can hurt parts of your growing brain. Looking at pornography is dangerous."

"Mom, if it's so dangerous, how do kids find it?"

"Many kids see it by accident on computers, phones, or other devices. Sometimes kids are shown pornography by another person—even by a friend or family member. Has that ever happened to you?"

I shook my head. "No."

"I'm glad. If that ever happens, will you come and tell me? I promise you won't get into trouble. It's just really important for me to know so I can help protect you."

"Sure, Mom . . . but I still don't understand why anyone would want to look at pornography."

Mom thought for a minute.

"It's normal for kids to be curious, and some kids are curious about pornography. For many kids, wanting to see pornography can feel like the pull of a giant magnet. After they see only one pornographic picture, their brains can be tricked into wanting to see more and more."

Mom put her hands on my shoulders and looked me in the eye.

"Part of my job is to warn you about danger. I've taught you to wear a helmet when you ride your bike to protect your brain on the outside. But pornography gets inside your brain and hurts it. Do you want to protect your brain on the inside, too?"

"I guess so. But how can pornography hurt my brain?"

"Pornography hurts your brain in at least two ways. First of all, it lies to your brain about how people should treat one another. It sometimes shows men being mean and even hurting women, and acting like it's for fun. Do you think being mean to others is a good way to have fun?"

"No way," I said.

Mom smiled and put her arm around my shoulders.

"But that's not all. Pornography can hurt your brain because looking at it can become a serious **addiction**. I want to tell you more about addiction, so *you* can protect *your* brain."

What did I learn?

Pornography is harmful pictures of people with little or no clothing on. Looking at it can cause two opposite feelings at the same time. Viewing pornography can be dangerous because it can trick your brain into wanting to see more pictures, which can then turn into an addiction.

NOTES

CHAPTER 2
What's an Addiction?

"Do you know what an *addiction* is?" Mom asked.

I pointed to a brownie sundae on the front cover of Mom's magazine. "Aunt Suzanne says she's addicted to chocolate," I said with a grin.

Mom smiled. "Some people joke about addictions, but a real addiction is a very serious problem. People whose lives are taken over by addictions are called *addicts*."

Mom's eyebrows scrunched together, and she thought for a minute.

"An addiction is like a powerful habit that is so strong most addicts feel they can't quit—even when they have tried really hard to stop. It feels like a trap they can't escape from."

"I remember Grandma used to smoke. Was she addicted?" I asked.

"Yes, she was. It took her many years to quit smoking. Other members of our family have struggled with addictions to alcohol or other drugs. But people can also become

addicted to behaviors like gambling or looking at pornography."

"Wow, people can become addicted to looking at bad pictures?"

"It's true. Some people become addicted more easily than others. But you *never* want to become addicted to anything, if you can help it."

"Why? What happens?"

"Most addicts make terrible choices that end up hurting themselves and the people they love. They often lie to hide their addiction from their friends and family. As they become more and more addicted, they can lose interest in their friends, school, and even having fun."

Mom sighed. "In fact, even with a doctor's help, most people find it extremely hard to recover from an addiction."

"Why is it so hard? Can't you just stop if you want to?"

"It's not that easy, and it all has to do with your two brains."

"Wait—I have *two* brains?"

Mom chuckled. "Actually, you only have one brain, but there are two major parts to your brain that are involved in addiction. We could call them the **feeling brain** and the **thinking brain**. Learning about your two brains can help protect you from addiction."

What did I learn?

An addiction is like being trapped in a very bad habit. Addicts often make poor choices and lie to cover up their addiction. Addiction involves two parts of the brain: feeling and thinking.

NOTES

CHAPTER 3

My Feeling Brain

Mom stood up and reached for a book from our bookshelf. Her fingers flipped through the pages until they landed on a picture of the human brain. We sat down at our kitchen counter to look at it.

Mom pointed at the picture. "Your feeling brain is right here in the center. It has several parts that work *automatically* to keep you alive. For example, when you go out to play on a very hot day, what happens?"

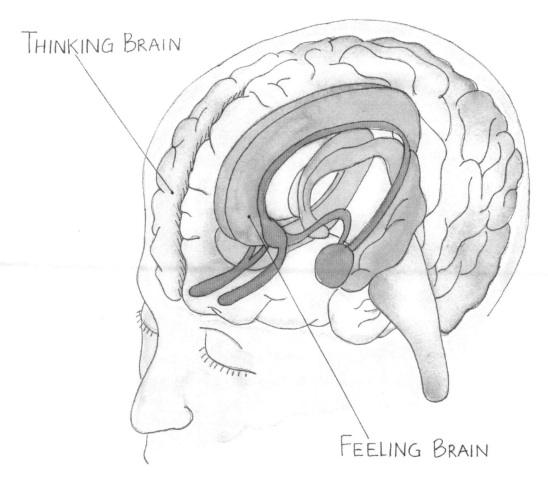

THINKING BRAIN

FEELING BRAIN

"I get sweaty."

"Right! That's your feeling brain sending a message to your body to help it cool down.

"What about when you go outside on a cold day without a jacket on?" she asked.

"I start to shiver."

"Exactly! That's your feeling brain sending a message to help your body warm up!"

"Your feeling brain is also in charge of basic **drives** that keep you alive. For example, the feeling brain makes you feel hungry and thirsty so you'll want to eat and get enough to drink. It has a special **reward system** that gives you a feeling of *pleasure* for doing things, like eating, that help you survive. Rewarding you with pleasure for doing important things is a big part of the

feeling brain's job."

"That must be why I like ice cream so much!"

Mom smiled. "Your feeling brain is necessary for your survival, but it also needs your help."

"Why?" I wondered.

"Because your feeling brain doesn't know right from wrong. It's kind of like a cheetah hunting a gazelle. Cheetahs kill gazelles for food—for them, it's not a matter of right or wrong, it's their survival instinct to kill when they're hungry.

"But humans are different from animals," Mom explained. "Humans have the ability to think about what they're doing, rather than always acting on their feelings."

"So the thinking brain is like a mom who tells a kid to stop eating too much ice cream," I joked.

"Exactly!" Mom winked, and we laughed together.

What did I learn?

My feeling brain is in charge of keeping my body alive. It makes me hungry, thirsty, and keeps my body at the right temperature. My feeling brain makes me want what it believes I need and then rewards me with feelings of pleasure for repeating those actions. But it's got one big weakness: it doesn't know right from wrong.

NOTES

_____

_____

_____

_____

_____

_____

_____

_____

_____

CHAPTER 4

My Thinking Brain

Mom tapped me on my forehead with her finger.

"This part of your brain, right here in front, is your *thinking* brain. It helps you solve problems, like doing your math homework or figuring out how to build a fort. Your thinking brain can make plans and exercise self-control, like when you control your temper. But more importantly, your thinking brain can learn *right from wrong*. It can learn how to make good choices because it remembers the consequences of bad choices. Your thinking brain can help you to stop, think, and make good decisions."

Mom pointed to a diagram of my thinking brain.

"Can you think of something your thinking brain helps you to do?" Mom asked.

I thought hard.

"Well, I've learned not to hit my brother when I get mad at him."

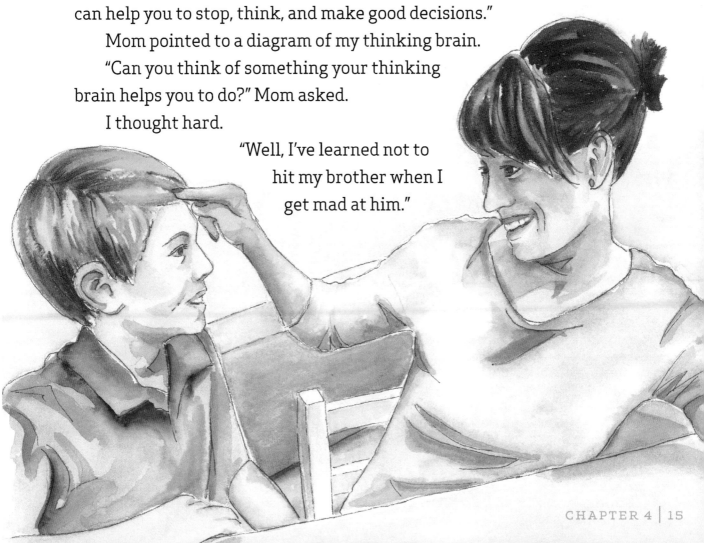

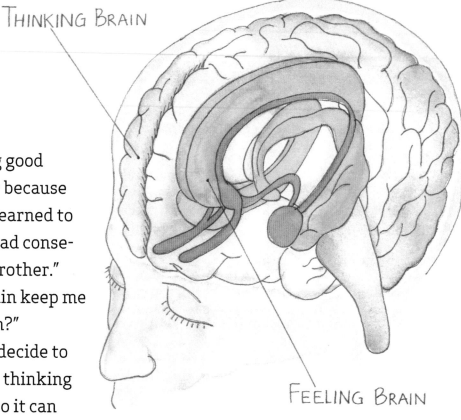

THINKING BRAIN

FEELING BRAIN

Mom smiled.

"Right. You're getting good at controlling your anger because your thinking brain has learned to stop and remember the bad consequences of hitting your brother."

"Can my thinking brain keep me from getting an addiction?"

"Yes. Every time you decide to make a good choice, your thinking brain becomes stronger so it can protect you from things like addiction. It's almost like exercising a muscle—the more you work it, the stronger it gets."

I flexed my arm. "I had no idea my brain can get strong like a muscle!"

Mom leaned over and hugged me. "Yes, you get stronger when you make good decisions."

What did I learn?

My thinking brain helps me solve problems, use self-control, and make smart choices between right and wrong, good and bad. By exercising my thinking brain, I can make it stronger!

NOTES

CHAPTER 5

My Two Brains Work Together

Mom stood up, and we walked over to a window that looked out onto our street.

"I'll give you an example to show how both brains can work together. Let's pretend it's a hot summer afternoon and you're hungry. An ice cream truck pulls up on the other side of our street."

She put up her left fist.

"Here's your feeling brain. It wants to eat, so it says, 'Go get the ice cream *right now!*'"

Mom put up her right hand. "But your thinking brain says, 'Stop! Look for cars first!'"

Mom brought her hands together, with her right hand covering her left fist.

"With your thinking brain in charge, your two brains can work together to keep you safe *and* help you get what you want. But what do you think happens if an addiction weakens your thinking brain so your feeling brain takes over making all the decisions?"

I thought for a minute.

"Well, I might run out into the street and get hit by a car . . . because I wouldn't *think* to look both ways."

"Right. Without your thinking brain, your feeling brain would do whatever it wants, even if it's not safe for you. So which brain needs to stay in charge?"

"My thinking brain!"

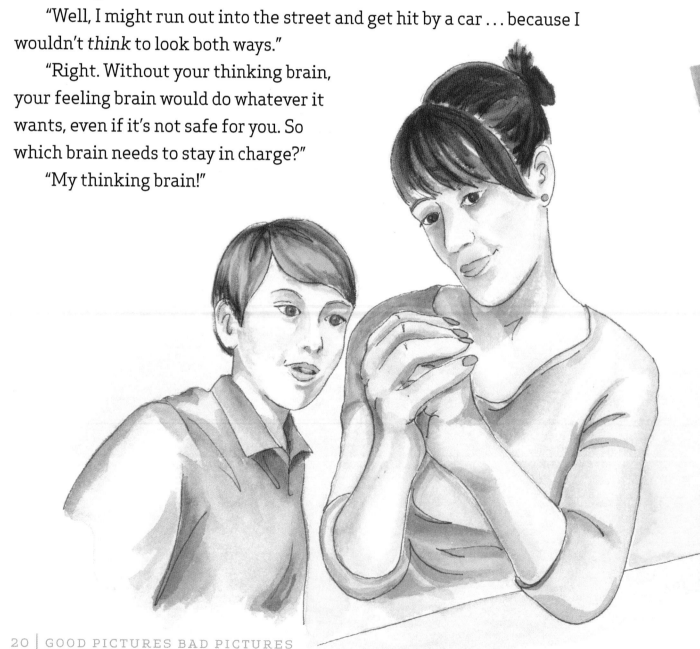

"Exactly." Mom nodded.

"Mom, all this talk about ice cream has got *both* my brains wanting some!" I laughed.

Mom smiled. "How about after dinner? You can help me get it ready, and we'll talk more about keeping our brains safe from addiction and pornography."

I wanted some ice cream right away, but I used my thinking brain to help me wait until after dinner.

What did I learn?

Both of my brains are important. But as I grow up, I need to make sure my thinking brain is in charge because my feeling brain doesn't stop to think before acting. I can stay safe by keeping my thinking brain in charge.

NOTES

_____

_____

_____

_____

_____

_____

_____

_____

CHAPTER 6
My Brain's Attraction Center

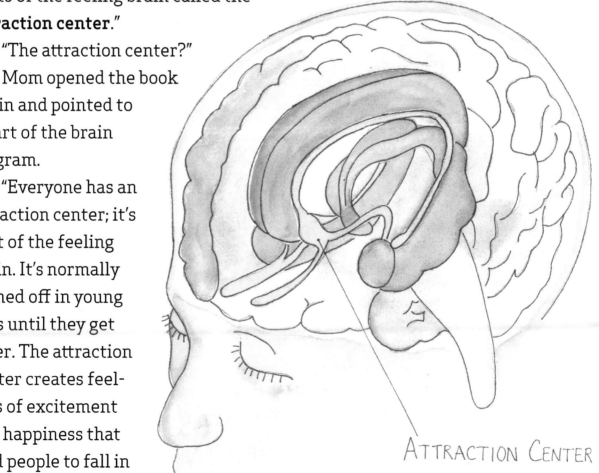

After dinner, Mom and I sat eating our ice cream at the kitchen table. After I finished my last spoonful, Mom asked, "Did you know that some people think a pornography addiction is harder to overcome than a drug addiction?"

"Really? Why?"

"One reason is because pornography fires up one of the most *powerful* parts of the feeling brain called the **attraction center**."

"The attraction center?"

Mom opened the book again and pointed to a part of the brain diagram.

"Everyone has an attraction center; it's part of the feeling brain. It's normally turned off in young kids until they get older. The attraction center creates feelings of excitement and happiness that lead people to fall in

ATTRACTION CENTER

love. It makes them want to be close to one another."

I rolled my eyes. "So why is *that* so important?"

Mom tousled my hair.

"Without the attraction center, moms and dads wouldn't be attracted to each other or want to get married. And if they didn't fall in love and come together, they wouldn't have babies. And if they didn't have babies, the human race might not survive . . . which means *you* wouldn't be here today!"

"Well, I guess that *is* important." I grinned.

"It's also important to understand that pornography tricks people into believing lies."

"What kinds of lies?"

"Watching pornography can lead you to believe that people are objects to *use* instead of real human beings with feelings. We know that everyone has feelings and wants to be treated with kindness, so that's one more way pornography lies to people who look at it."

"But don't people know the pictures aren't real? How can it hurt to watch people who are just acting?"

"Good question. The attraction center is designed to bring *real* people together, but it can't tell the difference between a picture and a real person. Looking at pornography *tricks* the brain into turning on very powerful feelings that are difficult to control, especially for kids. And that can become a big problem."

Mom picked up my brother's toy race car from off the floor. "Pretend this car is real. The *gas pedal* is like the attraction center. The *brakes* are like the thinking brain. What would happen if you pushed the gas pedal to the floor *and* the brakes weren't working?"

"I would crash and get hurt."

"Right. Pornography is dangerous because viewing it can put the feeling brain and its attraction center in charge of driving *you*, a long time before your thinking brain has strong enough brakes to control those kinds of feelings. And that can lead to developing an out-of-control addiction."

Mom handed me the race car. "So what are *you* going to do if you run into bad pictures?"

"I'm going to keep my thinking brain in charge by not looking at pornography."

Mom smiled again and put her arm around my shoulders. "I'm so proud of you for making smart choices!"

What did I learn?

My attraction center is part of my feeling brain. It's extremely powerful because it has a very important job—to bring moms and dads together to create families. But pornography can trick my attraction center and turn it on too early, before my thinking brain has the brakes to control it. That's why I need to stay away from bad pictures.

NOTES

CHAPTER 7

How Pornography Tricks the Brain into an Addiction

Mom and I got up from the table and worked together to do the dishes.

"Mom, do you think a kid could get addicted after seeing just one bad picture?"

"Most kids won't, but some kids who aren't prepared might get hooked very quickly."

"How does that happen so fast?"

"I'll try to explain. Pornography tricks the brain into releasing a big dose of chemicals that make the person watching it feel good, at least for a while. The scary thing about a pornography addiction is that the brain is tricked into making its own drug!"

"Really?"

"Yes. Many scientists now believe that looking at pornography can affect the brain in the same way as taking a strong drug. Using pornography may even shrink part of the brain!"

"That's scary!"

"Right! You already know never to try illegal or harmful drugs, but in some ways pornography can be worse. Although a drug addiction is very hard to overcome, at least the body has a way of getting rid of the drugs within a few days. Unlike drugs in the body, the brain can't get rid of pornography. Once you see those shocking pictures, they will always be there for you to remember."

"That's not fair!"

"No, it isn't. But once someone gets interested in looking at pornography, their attraction center produces intense **cravings** to look for *new* bad pictures. A craving is a strong desire for something, which means you want it so badly it's hard to think of anything else."

"So the attraction center wants to see more pornography? Why?"

"Because the brain gets bored with old stuff and excited by new stuff. Do you remember the last time you got excited about something *new*?"

"That's easy! My remote control truck I just bought. It took me a long time to save up for that!"

"Good example!" Mom said with a smile. "Now, do you remember when something new became kind of boring?"

I reminded Mom about the Crime Buster Detective Kit I got last year. I dreamed about it for weeks before my birthday, but now I almost never play with it.

Mom nodded. "It's the same with pornography. When pictures become boring, people look for even more shocking pictures and videos in order to feel the same level of excitement they did at first. Searching for and finding new and more extreme forms of pornography is what feeds an addiction."

"Wow! I don't want an addiction to happen to me!"

"Me neither. The problem is that seeing pornography very quickly creates a feeling of excitement in your body, even before you can turn away. It takes less than a half a second. And seeing even one picture can lead a kid to be super curious about pornography. The good thing is that *you can choose* to put the brakes on those feelings of excitement and curiosity *before* they grow into an addiction."

"How?"

"Great question!" Mom tapped the front of her head. "Your thinking brain can do it—it just needs a plan!"

What did I learn?

Memories of pornography can lead to intense cravings to see more pictures or videos, but the brain can quickly become bored. An addiction gets started when people search for new and more intense pornography in order to get their attraction center excited. To avoid an addiction, the thinking brain needs a plan.

NOTES

CHAPTER 8
My Thinking Brain's CAN DO Plan!

Mom said I should do my very best to stay away from pornography. But if I ever come across pornography, here's what I CAN DO.

Close my eyes.
Always tell a trusted adult.
Name it when I see it!

Distract myself with something different.
Order my thinking brain to be the boss!

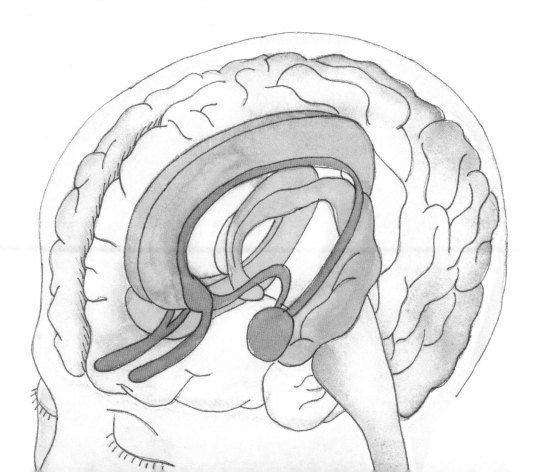

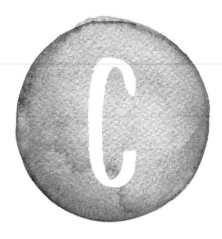

Close my eyes immediately.

Seconds count with bad pictures, and the longer I look, the stronger the memory becomes. After I close my eyes, I can *turn away*. If I'm on the Internet, I can turn my device off without looking at the screen. Turning it off is better than trying to close the website.

Always tell a trusted adult.

Keeping pornography a secret is never a good idea. Mom says the bad image may actually bother me more if I keep it to myself. If it's too hard to talk about, I can always leave a note. That way my mom or dad will know to find a time when we can talk.

And if I'm ever at a place where someone shows me pornography, I can use a secret code phrase (like "my stomach feels strange") to alert my mom or dad to come and get me.

Name it when I see it

Say quietly, but out loud, "That's pornography!" whenever I see a pornographic image. Naming it helps my thinking brain to know what it is and reject it.

Our family has decided to help each other recognize pornography when we see it. Even if we're out in public, we can quietly whisper to each other, "That's pornography!"

Distract myself

Distract myself with something different that is positive, interesting, or requires physical effort. When an image is bothering me, I can distract myself by doing something physical, like riding my bike, taking the dog for a walk, or playing a fun game with a friend.

Mom told me that some kids recite an encouraging poem, sing a fun song, or, if they follow a faith tradition, say a prayer to get their minds turned away from pornography.

I can train my thinking brain to focus on something different whenever a bad picture pops up in my thoughts. I can choose to pay attention to something else. With *practice*, those bad pictures will bother me less and less.

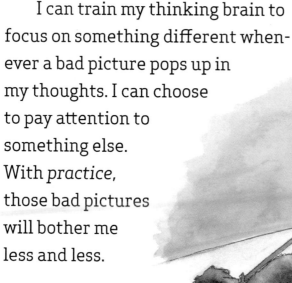

Order my thinking brain to be the boss!

I can decide to never, ever go looking for more pornography, even after I've been exposed to it. A good way to order my thinking brain to be the boss is to make it talk to my feeling brain.

"Feeling brain, you may be curious to see more bad pictures, but I am choosing to use my thinking brain to stay free from pornography."

I CAN DO this! I can make my thinking brain strong by deciding not to view pornography and by learning to control my thoughts.

CHAPTER 9

I Can Escape the Poison of Pornography

The next day after dinner, Dad and I hurried into the garage to work on my bike.

"Hey, I heard you and Mom were talking yesterday about *bad pictures*."

"They're called pornography, Dad."

Dad smiled. "Well, your mom's right—pornography is bad for the brain."

He picked up a wrench, and we started working on my bike. After we finished adding a new seat and handles, it looked brand-new!

"Thanks, Dad, it looks awesome!"

I took it for a ride and then came whizzing back and parked it in the garage. After we put away our tools, Dad pulled out a box from a locked cabinet and held it out for me to see.

"Do you know what this is?" he asked.

I looked at the label. "Is it poison?"

"Yes, it is. These chunks of bait are very tasty to rats, and they mistake them for food. But after a few bites, the poison begins to kill them."

Dad put the poison back into the cabinet and locked it shut.

"Pornography is a lot like poisonous bait. In fact, people who sell pornography put it on the Internet, TV, signs, and in magazines to try to trick you. At first, pornography might seem like a good idea because it can feel so exciting to your body. But sooner than you think, it can damage your brain, a lot like a poison."

"Mom said that if I ever see bad pictures, I need to say, 'That's pornography!' and then get away from it fast."

"That's right. If the rats could say, 'That's poison!' and then run away from it, do you think it could hurt them?"

"No, I guess not."

"If you recognize the pornography bait

out there and stay away from it, you'll be able to keep your brain safe."

Dad gave me a big hug.

"Remember our saying: If you make good choices *today*..."

"Good things will happen tomorrow!" I chimed in. I'd heard Dad say that a thousand times, and we both laughed.

"Anytime you want to talk, I'm here for you, okay?"

"Thanks, Dad."

Mom opened the door to the garage and smiled. "Hey, let me take a picture of you two with your latest project."

Mom's camera clicked and flashed.

Dad opened the kitchen door for us and turned off the garage lights. "Come on. I don't know about you, but I'm ready for dessert."

A pan of warm brownies sat on the kitchen table, and we all took turns sliding them out with a spatula.

Mom passed around her digital camera to show us the photos she'd taken of me and Dad.

Mom smiled. "These are *good pictures* to add to our family photo

album. They'll make great memories."

As I looked at the photo of Dad and me, I knew that *this* was the kind of picture I wanted to have in *my* brain.

When it comes to pornography, I want to be in control by using my thinking brain. And now I know I CAN DO it.

MY CAN DO PLAN

 **C** — Close my eyes immediately

 **A** — Always tell a trusted adult

 **N** — Name it when I see it

 **D** — Distract myself

 **O** — Order my thinking brain to be the boss!

Glossary of Key Terms

Addiction: An addiction is a chronic disease of the brain's reward system. A dysfunctional reward system creates strong cravings for the addictive substance or behavior, which cause addicts to lose control and compulsively seek it out despite negative consequences. Addicts develop tolerance, so they require more intense levels of stimulation for satisfaction and they experience withdrawal if they cannot use their addictive drug or engage in their addictive behavior. Most addicts experience cycles of relapse and remission. Without treatment, addictions are progressive and can result in disability or premature death.

Attraction Center: The structures of the brain involved in sexual attraction and arousal.

Chemicals: Substances made of tiny parts called atoms and molecules. The chemicals in the brain are like signals that carry messages from one part of the brain to another.

Cravings: Cravings are strong desires. More than a hunger, a craving is a powerful longing for something specific. Cravings can be so overwhelming that they wake addicts up during the night from a sound sleep.

Drive: A powerful need or instinct that motivates behavior, like hunger or sexual desire.

Feeling Brain: The limbic region of the brain responsible for our emotions as well as our survival instincts and feelings of pleasure. Memory and learning are also involved with the limbic system.

Pornography: (Simple definition) Pornography means pictures, videos, or even cartoons of people with little or no clothes on. (Advanced definition) Any kind of media—like pictures, videos, songs, or stories—that is designed to arouse sexual feelings by showing nudity or sexual behavior.

Reward System: The parts of the brain involved in creating feelings of pleasure or satisfaction to reward behaviors important for survival. An addiction corrupts the reward system so that it rewards addictive behaviors that are not helpful for survival.

Thinking Brain: This area of the brain is called the prefrontal cortex and is responsible for putting the brakes on the appetites of the limbic system. The prefrontal cortex learns right from wrong and can make plans and solve problems. It may shrink in size as the addiction transfers strength and control to the limbic system (or feeling brain). A few ways to fortify the prefrontal cortex include focused meditation, exercising self-discipline, and acting on plans to achieve goals.

Resources for Parents and Professionals

RECOMMENDED READINGS

Hilton, Donald L., Jr. MD. "Slave Master: How Pornography Drugs and Changes Your Brain." *Salvo Magazine*. Edition 13. 2010. http://www.salvomag.com/new/articles/salvo13/13hilton.php.

Kastleman, Mark B. *The Drug of the New Millennium: The Science of How Internet Pornography Radically Alters the Human Brain and Body*. Provo, UT: Powerthink Publishing, 2007.

Maddex, Bobby. "The Naked Truth: An Interview with Dr. Judith Reisman." Dr. Judith Reisman website. September 8, 2010. http://www.drjudithreisman.com/archives/2010/09/the_naked_truth.html.

Manning, Jill C., PhD. *What's the Big Deal about Pornography? A Guide for the Internet Generation*. Salt Lake City, UT: Shadow Mountain, 2008.

McIlhaney, Joe S., Jr. MD and Freda McKissic Bush, MD with Stan Guthrie. *Girls Uncovered: New Research on What America's Sexual Culture Does to Young Women*. Chicago: Northfield Publishing, 2011.

Muller, Mary. *The Guardians of Innocence, A Parent's Guide to Protecting Children from Pornography*. Bountiful, UT: Horizon Publishers, 2011.

ORGANIZATIONS & WEBSITES

www.ProtectYoungMinds.org

www.EducateEmpowerKids.org

www.EndSexualExploitation.org

www.Enough.org

www.FightTheNewDrug.org

www.PornHarmsResearch.org

www.WhiteRibbonWeek.org

www.WomenForDecency.org

About the Contributors

KRISTEN A. JENSON

Protecting kids became Kristen's passion after she received a late-night phone call from a traumatized mother dealing with the tragic consequences of her porn-addicted son. Since then, Kristen has become a best-selling author, a frequent speaker, and a guest on podcasts, webinars and radio broadcasts. She actively blogs at ProtectYoungMinds.org and serves on the Coalition to End Sexual Exploitation Prevention Task Force. Kristen is the mother of three (really great) kids and lives with her (really supportive) husband and (extremely cute) doggie in the beautiful state of Washington. She has a BA in English Literature and an MA in Organizational Communication.

GAIL A. POYNER, PHD

Dr. Poyner is a Licensed Psychologist and owns Poyner Psychological Services. She provides therapy for a spectrum of psychological disorders for children and adults, including pornography addiction and prevention counseling and currently serves as the President of the Oklahoma Psychological Association. Gail has six children and seventeen grandchildren (and counting!), and lives with her husband in Oklahoma. She enjoys working in the yard, as well as cheering for her beloved NBA Oklahoma City Thunder basketball team.

CLAUDINE GALLACHER

Claudine holds a master's degree in English with an emphasis in composition and rhetoric. She has been involved in the creation of *Good Pictures Bad Pictures* from the onset. She has served as a writing coach and research assistant to the authors, helped organize and gather feedback from the parent/child testing of the book, and has worked in the background to promote the goals of the Protect Young Minds blog. Claudine enjoys reading, doing genealogy, exploring the outdoors, and spending time with her husband and three children. She lives in beautiful Santa Barbara, California.

DEBBIE FOX

Debbie holds a bachelor's degree from Brigham Young University where she started as an art major and has continued her art education through community classes. Debbie lives with her husband in Washington State and is the mother of five children and contented grandmother of five (and counting!). In her free time she loves to exercise, travel (especially to visit her family) and let her creative juices flow.

Book design by Evan MacDonald